COLLECTION 2021 POEMS ALL

In heaven will I be allowed

to bog through salt marsh again?

MUCH NEEDED POEMS

from

CREEKLY SPEAKING

THE REST WITHIN

AN ECHAW REVERENCE

CONSIDERING

William Baldwin

Baldwin, William P. Much Needed Poems

Published by Evening Post Books, Charleston, South Carolina.

ISBN-13: 978-1-929647-90-3

Cover and interior design by Chance Taylor

ACKNOWLEDGMENTS

Most of these poems appeared, at least in some form, on my
Facebook site the morning they were written or the day following.
And I came to depend on the enthusiastic support I found there.
Again to those reading them: thank you.

For the actual editing of poems and with an appreciation far
beyond mere words, I'd like to thank Julia Kendall, Harlan Greene,
Nan Morrison, and Stephanie Waldron. And thank you wondrous
first reader and wife, Lil. For helping to lay out the book thanks to
my sons Aaron Baldwin and Malcolm Baldwin. For companionship
on walks and paddles and at meals thank you to my many friends,
especially Johnny Galbary, Susan Hindman, Dan Lesesne, Patty
and Jim Fulcher, Susan Kern, Chad Gerald, Sherry Browne, and
Patrick Klim, and Kathy Livingston. For guidance Rev. Jennie
Olbrych, Rev. Roy Hills, Rev. Callie Walpole and Annie Banks. At
the Village Museum a special nod to Bud Hill and Randy McClure
and the same to Hampton Plantation's Jayson Sellers and Hannah
Marley. For faith in the poetry writing projects thanks to editor/
publishers Alex Moore, Linda Ketron, Aida Rodgers, Richard
Wyndham, John Burbage, and Michael Nolan. And for a fine
layout thank you Chance Taylor.

INTRODUCTION

MUCH NEEDED POEMS are just that: the poems of four small books published since January of 2021. I had a stroke the January before, a near-death experience, and uncertain of the future, printed what came in forty poem increments. This is a diary of sorts. And a progression of thoughts.

Happily, I've written many well received books, each in its way a treatment of the complex beauty, apparent turmoil, and downright mystery of our existence. I hope what you hold in your hand is no exception.

March of 2020 'til now: turbulent days. The coronavirus brought shelter-in-place to our McClellanville, South Carolina. Economic uncertainty was suddenly upon us. Nightmarish racial conflicts caused outrage, not only in America, but the entire world. Chaos seemed the order of the day. But this village is relatively isolated, of course connected by computers, and the rest. The virus did arrive. Many were ill, but few required hospital stays. Some months ago my wife Lil and I received Covid shots. The church is open. Schools too. Joe Biden is now a well-established President. I have colon problems. Coming up is a cataract operation. Still, I ponder away and write daily. And when health permits, I continue to walk and paddle in the 300,000 acres of surrounding wilderness. Hope this brings you peace and pleasure. B.

CREEKLY SPEAKING

thank you's

to these old friends:

Susan Hindman

Dan Lesesne

Walter Shockley

Johnny Galbary

JOURNEY

Don't be surprised
when a solution
to the puzzle comes
ahead of the question
asked: a ready is
before the by and by,
words teetered,
now low, now high,
the crisscross dipping
of a kayak paddle,
the steady straddle
which is both arriving
and skedaddle.

THE CAMELLIAS

Pretend it's a wilderness
and all around you this,
what life has built,
is built from scratch:
the growing storm, the rising void,
the curse of plague, the unemployed,
the whisper: This and this and this avoid.

NEW DAY:

I wish for us the quiet things,
the broad expanse, the can't explains.
I wish for us the elsewhere whats,
the right here cares and everywhere
a world immune, a peace at last,
and not that wound of words
ballooned above some cartoon head.
Yes, instead, my friends,
with just a touch of pain, may
"Pray, Patience, Love"
be inked in blood
across our hearts
these starts of each new day.

THEM

From the attic dormer window,
the one to the furthest right,
from there, by growing tall,
the child could spot the old Cape Light,
where, more than once, his grandpa,
with a young man's nerve
climbed over the final rail,
followed a fool hero's urge —
by way of lightning rod
was led to the cupola's roof
to stand unaided on his head.
He laughed there in his fearless proof.

He's seen the world from upside down:
beach, creeks, marsh, wide bays,
earth above, heaven below,
an endless round of ocean waves.
And all this is his.
He keeps odd universe alone.
Then having done it for awhile,
descends to tend his own
mother's cow and catch
a supper's worth of trout.
And him an old man now,
who bent still rows his bateau out.

JAY SINGS TO MARTHA

Yes, hear the whispered roll of surf.
Across the dunes wait eye made moons.
In such a light wild stars grow dim.
Not knowing night the Kinglet sings
and on the breeze warm breath of salt.

When we are done and gone from here,
may God our hair to cirrus spin
and use our pulse to stir the stars, then
let four moons our eyes supply
to bright strange nights of four moon skies.

DAY CLEAN

Salt waves swing,
fold up and flee.
Seems ebbing's
got the best of me.

Porpoise sighs,
porpoise rolls,
first gull glides
and first gull scolds.

The sun's a fire
of quiet red.
By quiet doubt
new day is edged.

Yet gaps beneath
bare heels now rise.
Let's trust in toes
to chase the tide.

PETAL, PISTIL, STAMEN

Each weed makes the weed mistakes
its trifling parents did.

Each flower blooms immaculate,
conceived of seed we've rid

of blame...Otherwise
they're much the same.

DOG SONG 8: THE CHALLENGE

As everybody's got something going on--
a mountain of ice they're climbing,
that long swim from Dover over--
we were lucky to find this quiet trying
of an undeveloped challenge, this simple
trip requiring only one of us
to shuffle to and from the percolator,
while the other rolls on his back,
waves his paws around,
and makes that snorting sound.

6

BIG WELL POND

I am too old to learn the name
of any new bird smaller and
less gaudy than an Eagle.
And here is no exception.
A foot tall nondescript wader.
Tired. Haggard even.
And, devoted to his stretch of marsh.
Hunt and peck: reminds me of me
searching for some common word
forgotten for the umpteenth time
I still think to find among the mind's
mud and crooked stems...Yet...
Then again, seen in better light,
this stilted little creature...Yes. Wait.
Why it's that magic ageless
and warm appetite for quiet
that even now stirs me with delight.
Nice. Nice.
A *Bird of Paradise.*

CROSSING THE BAR: for Helen M.

All we have is dust to dust.
Nothing left of hearts but trust.
Azaleas, grave, some coffin screws,
yet still we hope for shrimping, too.
Boats with stainless through and through.
Cypress planked and fastened new.
Along the pilings walkway hung
where to the waists the lines are strung,
and all in Heaven creaks and sways
in imitation of fall days,
for this is Holy's measure:
The storms 'round there are
off on stars,
and waves are light,
the mornings bright,
each tow a dream
of treasure.

HIGH ABOVE

Those forgotten by Noah and his wife,
hence missing the Ark,
angry and/or sad
were forced to swim,
their furry clawed paws or
flailing hooves
churning up a foaming sea.
All this still found today
in drifting clouds
which, free of gravity,
remind me: whatever it is,
I need to be at it.

PLANTATION RUINS

Masons stuccoed laid brick
and scored this so it'd look like stone.
Large mock-blocks of granite floated
up the Santee and wrestled into place
by black men enchanted with their
servitude. In harmony 'round us now
magnolia, hickory, holly, too,
though roaring HYDRO-AX
has ripped you limb from limb,
take hold. Again silent,
beauty bound, renew:
grow. We're through.

THE HAMPTON PLANTATION DIG

This way and that, a trench we've dug
to find a way past fear,
some foreignness
that we have missed
and dream is buried where
turned earth inhales,
gives a sigh, and next a wail.
Left so long pine roots impale
thick crumbled bricks of chimney,
hearth and piers,
and ghosting children lose the way
back to this house of slavery days.
Or do they?
Hear those laughing feet?
And there is rain on cypress shakes
and thunder makes them stand
stock still and wait.

VOYAGER

Back sprang aside pushed I
the branch I pushed aside
sprang back, erasing fast
the paddle's stroke, and
with it curse unspoken.
For grunt, then laugh's
enough to measure this
displeasure with myself
and a banging thorny path.

SUPPER

Seeing blue-willow spread
of fried fish and buttered grits,
the voice in my stomach calls
to the hand I hold the fork with…
actually it whispers as the mind
mutes such messages,
makes 'em sound distant, like
coming from the flesh's
equivalent of an earlier time's
dimly-lit antique kitchen, where
at a round oak table, I bow
my head in racing prayer.

THE PRESBYTERIANS

When Auntie bent her head and crooned
the words: "The Old Gray Goose is dead",
the rockers of the creaking chair
rose and fell against a floor which led
not just to bed but through Jerusalems.
Steps worn with ancient humming rhyme,
my blanketed sister held in pink, pink
frayed silk in shining dipping line.

GOING TO DIG POTATOES

Captain Ben fixed two whale bones,
huge circular vertebra, to the garden's fencing,
thus giving something' of a nautical heroic
 motif to the yard, which is only fair since he
risked the government fine and stink of rotten
whale to bring 'em here. And each year
the sunflowers grow tall, brown faced,
and bending towards the middle part of June,
inquire across the wire squares:
Who are these giants that bloomed so soon?

IN LIEU OF WALKING THE FISH POND

There is a path
of stepped on grass,
wild matted stuff
pressed down enough.
But stepping winter
lays it further.
Him, with bare limbs,
inured to things
which tremble
we the sensible.
Aging us, fresh
to nothing less
than death,
but capable of
humming some.

HONEY HILL TRAIL

Both booted feet
splash scrambling
cross the muddy bottom
of the narrow creek
you thought with grace to leap.
Arms wave, you are sinking.
All the while, neither wet nor cold,
on the far bank, almost
eye level waits, smiling
with your face, that wild
"what was I thinking"
 goal of flying.

CONCERNING BIRDS

Salutations and lamentations:
another bird has up and flown.
See those wild soaring feathers.
He/she, with crest, feet and beak grown
unique, has me leap-looking in the book,
'cause what is missed does mystery stay.
Fumbling through the pages, thumbing on from Auks
to Zebra Hawks, for in my eyes each day
an unknown river's born.
To its far shore they have gone.

DUNKY BUILDS A BATEAU

When Dunky built the Duchess
it was a gentler time.
The Beatles were together.
Ancient craftsmen took their time.

Every nail he drove
was twice dipped galvanized.
Every line of bateau
pure balm to sorey eyes.

At something like a point
he bent the frame to fit.
Full inch oak but green —
there was no need to soak it.

The sides were yellow pine,
the bottom cypress planks,
the Duchess sealed with roofing tar
and cotton pulled from hanks.

Gray paint was Navy surplus
left over from past war out there.
The bottom red to waterline,
worm proof and drawn with care.

Then where the best is hidden,
that's where old Adam slipped her,
to pick five bushels every day
of handsome hand-size oysters.

TRANQUILITY

The hiss of mallards dropping in:
the muted splashes
followed by a garble boasting
of satisfaction, all hidden
then by persistent mist.
And being human
and not a duck,
I'd been struck by the coldness,
of my hand's featherless
flesh, and fumble now
a steaming thermos cup,
as gun, neglected, rests
in cradle arm, for such is thirst.

CAROLINA BAY

This lush swamp garden where I paddle
was, a mere twelve thousand nine hundred
years ago, a steaming hot vapor-shrouded
meteor-driven crater, a wasteland dead
to all things, but at present filled with
dark water where on every hand,
fringed by white water lilies,
monumental cypress do rise,
the pock's high rim of overthrown
and twisted things now built
to a sand-floored scented pine forest.
All this as if to show we who visit here,
the world might build on that soil's
memory, through regeneration
ignore the shove of hungry
nations, mend itself.

CHICKEN CREEK POEM

My recent being lost
cost me no more than a few
panicked thoughts,
a desperate sequencing of events
immediately preceding paddling
into a deeply flooded but motionless
elbow of a tupelo swamp,
from which a small, silent-flighted
owl dismissed itself,
as the sun, gone behind thick clouds,
had done already.
This leaving me to the creek's trickery,
to the trees' trickery,
to the menace of my many years,
circling, circling to the spot
of my loss's beginning, 'til
spying a frail fallen hickory leaf
sailing triumphant on a finally
noticed current.
The swamp no more an iron box.
All it took's a try.
And so it is with poems.
But not in quite that way.
They slog ashore, come singing,
ring themselves half dry.

A SEA POEM

There's a building in Atlanta
where they go to see the whale
and wonder at the shimmer
of the fishes' flashing scales.

No way you can tell 'em,
those of inner lands,
the sea's an old and wrinkled thing
who seizes all she can.

She wears a cloak of feathers,
some blue, some green, some white,
and skims across the minds of men
with talons shining bright.

What? She's other things as well?
A home of gods? A moon-thick tide?
Great salty place to float a boat
or walk the dog beside?

Okay. I guess that's so.

THE WAY

The going places where
wild things have run
walked or crept
do appear vaguely
worn, hollow, swept,
and we follow them
with careful, narrow,
snake-watch steps,
all the while,
slapping flies,
and trusting in the
trusting human way,
our stories coincide
with those of deer
and cautious rabbits.

THE BEND IN FIVE FATHOM

Who are you?
Who have you been
becoming since out on
that gloriously desolate
Isle of Skye the first
of your ancestors
invented the famed Scottish wheel
and set it rolling into the icy sea?
An event memorialized today
by, above November's
gold tipped marsh,
laced in the bluest sky,
a parade of drifting white clouds,
and these, unencumbered by gravity,
remind me by tumbling,
whatever it is I need to be at it.

IN MEMORIAM

A long way down,
which is why my sons nailed
garden fencing under this top rail
of their parent's back deck.
And there, wanting to get closer
to some indifferent cat,
the yapping dachshund
would stick his narrow nose
through small rectangles
of the lowest rows:
each now a silent wire void.

AU NATUREL

We know a roosting Barred Owl
isn't always melancholy.
"Who" from chest, up from belly,
not pure stuff of lost or folly.

Just ownership by sound,
an invitation to a mate,
who loves back with love complete,
but revels still in mock debate.

For both are confident, at least,
of a firmness in God's earth,
and, through joys of wild being,
certain of their spritely worth.

ANOTHER NIGHT LETTER

A small tin-roofed, built on stilts,
wet, green house, settled in
a slightly bigger pool of wet
security light with its bright fringe
of dripping trees, and past that
a far grander smudged stars
Universe of Whatness. That storm
is gone. Our seemed to be start
of a hurricane, wild, howling wind
rain ruckus is probably by now
in the sea off Morehead City. Been
gone and the power stayed on. How?
And me, waking far before dawn,
am fortunate to have, from last year,
porch strung ornamental Christmas
bulbs up and needing to shine here.

CREEKLY SPEAKING

It may sometimes
suit our porpoises
to see 'em as frisky
sea-going horses.
They whinny and blow,
and before you know,
with wavy manes,
are bucking away,
bucking away.
Down the creek they go.

DEVIOUS

Disguised with a finger mullet
dangling by its breathing lips,
the sharp hook, if cast into the creek,
appears edible to trout, fishes
which lack discernment, the real
in this case confounded by
rods bending, our smiling faces.
And we, with believing eyes,
draw strength in each arrival.
And each tossing back:
each contest of survival

EXPECTATIONS

At birth the buried acorn knows at once
which way is up, 'cause it's a fact:
the busy winter-fearing squirrel left in earth
a trail of chattered *coming back*.

the rest within

For Lil

TO UNDERSTAND

That's broke already.
Do not bend.
Do not staple.
Life's been pinned.
Fruits of labor
pulped then canned.
Yet at each halt
let's laugh. Begin.

BESIDE THE SEA

Ankle deep or less
for wading shallows
and being the cautious
squeamish sort I know
not to prod a still jellyfish
with my bare toe,
but,
like three gulls snatching at
a ragged morsel,
each to pull in its direction,
let's have poems
open to suggestion.

DAWN

Across a broad and curving earth
the first of the sun has found its way
to where gas station burned away
to press against the pumps that stayed.
And what can be learned from
a meter's face, what's frozen
on wheels that once have traced
the gallons, prices, such lifelong things.
Alive, Alive. Alive, Alive, O.
Far less I'm expecting than
ancient eyes show.

THAT WAMBAW ROAD PRAYER

Self said and self consumed,
Cardinals woken fall to
shaping chortles, chirps
which in likely truth,
make nothing happen.
Still some humans
standing on the road to listen,
do say to birds—
if in not so many words:

Tilt up the day,
drag up the light, scrape
the bottom of the night.
In your unrestraint of voice.
teach again to breath, rejoice.

AN UNFOLDING

With up and down of coffee cup
in whispered hiss an answer came.
Some separateness is real and wet:
the dripping eaves, a sky to drain.
We're locked in hour's uncertainties, so
I am where I need to be. The rain the same.
At least, that's how it seems

MEMORIES OF SUMMER DAZE

Forget the tanned asleep at the beach
and shaded dog who panting lays.
It's the upright laboring ones
who sweat beneath a frying sun.
Sun less than kind, world astride,
round, roaring yellow like some grand
thrown there egg done sunny side.

UNCLE WEWA

Stood within the common information,
the grid of narrow tree-lined streets,
several well-steepled churches,
plus our rambling stretch of shrimp docks,
with teaching linked to breathing,
the occasions for education
varied and constant, not surprising
how I can still hear I'd tied that boat
up like a cow.

WHEN: for Aunt Mary

The things
some women will do
to protect their chickens
are truly of another time.
To save their favored fowl
they'll still swing an axe
at a Great Horned Owl.
Or even attack with a thin
leaf rake a bright-mouthed
huge lunging snake.
And not just the hens.
The roosters, too.

THE CROSSING DREAM

One tragic night
it came aloose,
got left behind
Old Red Caboose,
and ended in the soybeans,
where still it dreams
its crossing dream
of being seen,
of children leaning
'tween their parents'
front-seat heads shouting,
how, at last, the train's complete.
Blinking lights cease,
the guard board is raised,
when its clacking retreats
into life's silence.

MILTON'S MANTIS

When we walk, we loom well seen,
by 3-D eyes of bugs which seem
to be just twigs or leaves, or such.
Unholy shapes as we would have it,
tiny tricksters, monster habits.
Pray they do, but not like us,
who wish a world more based on trust
and need pure beauty steadfast, just.

A MAYDAY PRAYER

I cannot die if I still move.
Blinking eye, whispered breath:
lingering death can't come to pass.
Let me use myself up sooner
kicking down some grassy path,
paddling black water creek...
or rocking in the porch's swing,
raising hands and, weak
from giving thanks, I cease.

SPECULATING IN MAY

I'm starting to suspect there're more
universes than the one 'round here.
You wonder. An infinite number?
Based on gratitude some quiet places
waiting inside this same horizon—
close by longitudes and latitudes
anchored in disremembered thankfulness.
How many just of blessedness?

ON MARVELS

Thus Pelican on soaring wings
begins a morning's work
by leaving below
a static sandy shore
for a high up feather folding
sudden drop followed by
a crashing,
half submerging stop.
Then floating marvel
raises bill so fishes
slide into its gullet,
a compartment
not found in us,
which, you see
(ah, surprise),
is why the Pelican's
bill will hold more
than its belly can.

SPRING AND REAL THINGS

There was always something
happening, something else
needed from the unthroned gods
and goddesses, as well.
Those unsettled ones who
even now roam amongst
the flitting warblers
of a cypress forest,
through a May garden
whose roses blaze,
or by some bright sliding
side-beach waves.
Why if we took the time and knelt,
(at least inside our heads) half-naked,
gauze drifting Spring herself,
unshod arch exposed
in dancing, might appear,
these solemn days barely
making head way 'gainst
the howling storm
born of how indifferent
we have grown to ancient beauty's
foreign pagan dreams, demanding
of our earth, a tilting on its
axis, endless spinning,
plus lingering of life well
past life's rightful seasons.

ON HOPE AND LOVING LIFE

Turns out the sun is spinning on its side,
meaning our earth's ride through the Milky Way
may hum both high and low and places have their
shorts and longs, with hope each day
drawn by us and by the Cardinal
or the Willet's song,
lighting up the woods,
the beach at dawn.

PITCH LANDING ROAD THINNING

This is how the years compute.
Where Wild Hog roots
and Flicker sings,
there we stop to count tree rings,
to read the cut pine's stump,
to watch the seasons jump and jump.
Summers wide, winters thin,
how we might look if seen in-
side: sorrows, joys, feast, and famine.

THE DAY WE DIE

The day we die
someone in flood control
will open up the great dam's gate,
raise the river to the point
our bogging prints are rinsed
away, for otherwise it'd
seemed we stayed. So someone
is the one who comes
to cover all the marks
we made and trade out words
for murmurs.

IKEA or Borders of a Solitude

How came these weary parts to me:
the broken throat, both ears deafened,
eyes dim, with mysteries shimmed?
Yep, life's arrived with bundled cares.
Thought's oblivious to fears,
all I think is: What goes where?

THE SUN AGAIN

I dreamed again last night
of writing poems which went
not unlike this one's going,
but these lines find a resolution,
while, with the baking sunlight
coming through the morning
window, what was inside
night head dries up
no matter how tight
I close my eyes.

LESSON

And there I was thinking
nothing's happened yet.
It's as if I brought the
watercolor set and wet
the brush and let my mind
drift across the waiting
space only to be met
by you, alive, waving.

THE WAMBAW WATCHERS

Busy warblers sing:
stand thin-legged, fold in wings,
tilt gold throats, invite, defend,
and all around wild world begins
to form of music's chipping
these courtships' outer rims,
which causes us to hold our breath:
Out. Then in.

ON SURPRISE

The requirements of astonishment
resemble those of amusement
in that surprise comprises
the major element of both.
Of course, the growth of wings
shucks order by the fistful.
Gravity pales. And soon,
not content with lowly drift,
shifting arm muscle gears
brings us within reach
of the highest pelicans,
boldest of the ring-billed gulls,
And there we share each bird's
thoughts of God, while dizzyingly
startling our fresh eyes
with a press of blue distances
and steady spread and sink of waves
upon as yet to be abandoned beach.

1694

To figure out
what witches
went where
once fled here
to old time Carolina's
Awendaw,
we need no more than
family trees and
the tests they do
with DNA's.
They'll show the ways
Salem's blood
arrives in us.
How demonic angels,
rustling cape
draped wings, hid
behind slab doors
on leather hinges.

BIRTHDAY ISLAND: for Cheves and Susie

The wake the outboard makes
takes waves in hand
and aims them at the shore,
where lapping shell, mud or sand,
whatever there's convenient,
the grinding of our continent
is done—well, a bucketful, no more.
And they, the waves, though
manufactured fairly small,
for a rushing moment
we must allow,
as in acknowledge,
perhaps a pride of purpose,
their place upon a cutting edge.

.

MY GRANNY'S TABLE

A pad of butter meltin',
sunken through the heat met with.
And leave room for fish:
two fresh croaker fried crisp.
All this writ large. God's
manifold and great mercy: grits.

RAINY DAY RHYMES

There is no sun. Eaves they dripped.
The rain grew wider, wetter yet.
Stretched itself 'til duplicates.
So, of course, again I fret then
another day in waiting spent,
which is when my smiling wife
goes and shakes her head.
"I said," she says, "You
have no patience. None."

THE REST WITHIN: for Dan

Just now afloat on the lily lake
and having eaten the last Nab,
that tasty, small, square, glaringly
orange, pattern-punctured cheese
cracker filled with a salty sweet
paste of peanut butter, I found
myself longing for another,
for this same food is the main
furniture of the Southern soul,
where for a short while, at least
and at best, it remains whole,
allowing our miniaturized inner
selves to plunk down, and on such
a mattress, stretch out and rest.

CREEK DAYS: for Bob

Let us be up and doing,
with a heart for anything.
Start long day of labor,
enjoy what labor brings.

But who needs a grand old poet?
No, nothing near sublime.
Just turn your face to cold stinging rain.
And pat wet knee to keep the time

WABI-SABI

Worn to a perfect luster,
my nose still rises to divide
two canted slits of smiling eyes,
these to see swift feathers fly.

Have laughing mouth and cheeks
to keep the barely working ears
stuck out there to hear sweet songs
sung among the broken leaves.

BEN AT THE CATSBY LILY

The very first symptom,
the very first if we don't count
our first heart thump and breath,
is that general unease
when pushing these old bones
from one stance to the next
complex even if relaxed pose.
Of course, the muscles help,
but the will, at heart, still must
do all that. Push and pull
us as a blindfolded child
at some old spinning game,
'til allowed to stop, stand
panting and see again.

AN ALCHEMY

Ancient live oak trees
which twisting meet
above a narrow asphalt street.
All empty 'til a fire truck tore
wailing, flailing moss from limbs,
blistering thoughts with yellow din:
This life, this life, this life, it roars.
Then comes a quiet. All the more.

BERKELEY COUNTY

The woods 'round here are in some trouble—
places where there's mostly stubble,
stubble, stumps on ancient dunes,
for oceans close by here have boomed,
where dragon creatures, many toothed,
frolicked, snorted, naught to lose,
and old storms rolled their waves upon
what humankind, as yet unborn,
could not covet, could not mourn.
Ancient wear, now fragile climate:
the shores of man are never quiet.

AWAY

Would I could share with you
a home-grown play of light on leaves.
A soft light found behind
old tired eyes.
No. Not a long way off —
Just across from here. I should say:
As the tiny bird flies.

THE SADLY TRUE POEM

When I've lost the dream of doing,
misplaced it as we must,
and not content with what's been done,
I've rummaged through life's stuff
for echo of a wanting, in vain for just beguns,
time enough to settle then for
All that's lost in Heaven's won.

MAY'S END

For no good reason
other than a shift in season seems
this bird seed currency is debased:
plastic tube feeder hangs disgraced.
But at least one Cardinal came.
Flitting there past the window glare.
Perhaps that was to mock. Him.
He cocked red-capped head, then
flew away to the Chinaberry tree
where the Chinaberry berries, bright
and ripe, weight the weaving limbs,
clearing my way to find a second cup of coffee,
and renew this posture of a sweet defeat.

PITCH LANDING STORK

The Wood Stork,
with its long dour face
and black trimmed
sloping cape,
had found a cypress
shrouded place,
if not to mourn,
at least to meditate,
which I in rattling truck
abruptly end. For that
distance pressed between
the careless smile of me
and cautious fly
away of him
is swollen fast, well past
all understanding.

SAND QUARRY STORK

The young Stork
on the other hand,
met me at the quarry
with his two girlfriends,
and took the station wagon's
bumper's reflection to be
a rival for his mates' affection.
He did a dance in the way of David.
Raised his wings, draped 'em so,
leaped and pranced around,
'til in hope of a better photo,
striving I rolled my window down.

THE PICKLE FACTORY

Beyond the sometime falling
Rust-pitted chain-link fence,
the stretch of unkempt weeds,
rise the soaring concrete walls,
of a grand century-old
abandoned pickle factory,
standing just so in contrast
to the surrounding small
well-tended houses, and as if
we need to share with God
the broken odd things in our hearts,
inside holding three full stories
 of a light-enhanced graffiti art.

ON PERMANENCE

Before this morning's pounding rain
we had a momentary permanence,
a pure stillness, with its willingness
of tree leaves not to shift,
the breeze to maybe whisper,
but with words so indistinct
I think: No, 'cept for the thunder's
grumble this is honest quiet.
Me, this house, this street, repeat.

AN ECHAW REVERENCE

For DIXIE: Mama to us all.

I AM

My first thought was to find
a piece of shore, one posted
or not, any place
with a sand and mud mix
firm enough to hold up my
old Croc wearing self,
and pick there a mess
of oysters.
Scratch some clams.
Just a few of each.
A bucket full which I am
lurching to the boat with
to sit, rest and imagine.

ON HEARING OF THE BEAR NEXT DOOR

If I am to be chewed up
and swallowed by a wild animal,
I wish it to be a furry warm mammal.
And have her a fit female nurturing
 a tumbling bunch of kits or cubs,
so that I will, as love, be again
and again partaken of.

AT DUTART CREEK: for Sherry

These plastic bottles have grown
to such an independence,
without caps somehow they float,
grouping thick among the dipping
willow branches, little buoy boat
selves boasting of voyages taken
and future trips they plan to make.

IT

Sit me down in silence,
Stand me up in praise,
From side to side
the ocean rolls,
sloshing in a bowl I made
of held out hands,
cup fingers raised.
Pile the sky on top.
Don't stop. Don't skimp.
Add a cloud.
Add a gull. Add two.
Pirouette 'em. Crowd
it in. Every bit.
A quick sound it.
Across the eye, the tongue
it fits, and will be heard.
as this it we hold
is spun from words.

FACE TO FACE

I turn my eyes from all
strange beautiful things
a TV screen can bring.
Hold at bay the jarring
of my mind,
the glamorous tube
though which eyes
move, and use
the quiet space up
gazing at that shadow
my forehead makes on
the glazed contents of
adjacent coffee cup.
Next a nod. A sip.
Mild exaltation
followed by a smile.
I send you this.

THE SHIP

Scratched though
and written in again is:
What can they hope to find
on that moon's dark side...
which I now finished with:
...not visible from here?
What worth-while
can reside back there,
what fate awaits, what grim
wisdom comes to
the him or the her,
the dazed who crash land in
time to wander through this line
and to we who on the firm earth,
stand in safety?

LETTING GO

Lose yourself between the "e"
of lose and "b" between the
"f" of your now unseen self
and first "e" of between's three,
hence finding that quiet
corner spelt of a sensible
silence.

REMEMBER THE REAL

Those bold juxtapositionings
of the seemingly ordinary plus
the purely fantastical elements found
usually just in paperback fictions
of magic realism,
these are the actual facts for cats,
who behind their casual masks
continually watch for strange
behavior—especially in humans.

HAMPTON BRAILLE

When Spring left us,
she left behind
prints in hardened mud
and petal strewn
decaying blooms,
things which Summer,
grown blindly thick,
divines a message in
and may take as his own.

DO IT

You look through the mirror
to the sheetrock beyond,
to the studs in the wall,
driven nails in the plate.
Don't wait for the ceiling
to fall into place,
the roof to renew,
or the sky to expand.
Loose from your eyes
the slackness of sleep.
A universe teeters
and smiling won't keep.

A WORLD 'ROUND HERE: for Larry

Setting the fresh scent
and long shadows aside,
any story I want to tell
about a Southern pine tree
could begin with a seed
and end with a stump,
and I'd fill the in between,
the growth, the felling,
with just an estimation
of board feet, of lumber
contained, but, trust me,
don't try explaining this
to the squirrels
or the woodpeckers.

FOR WE BIRDERS

I can't but could if blessed with wings
and claws to wrap branch tight,
aggravate a troop of us
by staying out of sight.

No way for me to camouflage
and sing among the leaves,
to disappear before our eyes:
for an encore boughs and leaves.

Yet hope I've got enough of art
to tease you to art's ends,
to pull you through imagined woods,
and craft a laugh to make amends.

THE FUEL DOCK

I am of two minds here:
one grinding out a line of poem,
the second more a launch in space,
a sprawling leap from off dock's end,
where on the creek leaked
fuel still floats, laps against
small patched shrimp boats.
Abyss of years—this
dash. Have upper case
for my young FACE,
and all the rest let
time erase.

VACATION PLANS

If I could think some other things,
turn some dial and changes bring
to what my neurons come upon,
what the synapses leaping join,
but the thoughts I have are
the aging thoughts I have:
my flying trailer trucks erupting
down a fuming Innerstate,
as I try to read at a steep angle
their vibrating sides.

JUST TO SAY

I pressed my thumb against the plum,
then spilt juice in my beard,
wiped this off with back of hand
and hand on shirt to show I cared
what others thought, at least the ones
who'd bit and found, with auspicious
sweet slurping sound—plus leaving
earth no worse for wear—
a knowledge pure delicious.

HAULING BACK

Hauling back we brought to the surface
all sorts of small, writhing, non shrimp
panting things—these facing death,
thus breached into the air. Yet most, instead,
go sliding through the scuppers
drop into the pitching sea,
escaping that bright trap plus
plunging birds, due as we all
should be a second chance,
a stepping clear
of life's unhingements
and their brushing
nets of words.

COFFEY SWAMP

First a grand stand
of bark stripped
sycamore, next
the flitting thrush,
then the beavers' stick built hut,
and stretches of
an ancient rice field
now treed again in tall
knot-kneed cypresses
and everywhere are tupelos.
The dike's broke through.
Oh, all here not unlike
some sad memory
of a graceless slavery and
an unforgotten war.
Another time so other place.
The deer dog and the deer escape.
Despite the woods and all
that grows there,
still a road and all
that goes where
leaping steel built
pickup trucks, wide
tired, high axles tear their
way through rutted mud,
as going on is
in the blood.

THAT GOLDEN SOLSTICE

Bless our souls,
for it's been told
rich in wisdom
are worn old men.
Yet on earth spins.
which plows us under,
pulls us in, and almanac
stays guide to spring.
Baking summer, on the
other hand, we tend
to understand.

THE GRACE OF POSSIBILITIES

The stars grow dim. They disappear
and take night's burdens off somewhere.
Plain earth's sufficient for my needs,
roads/creeks 'round here my galaxies.
And if God behind my back is smilin',
I pray now: More power to Him.

FATHER'S DAY 2021: for Rev. Roy

Finding a deer in just thin air
requires imagination.
But finding four,
a whole deer nation,
points to wildest
speculation.
Lying cornstalks,
treasonous leaves,
oh, father gone
come stand by me,
smile, lift your hand,
and white-tails raise.
Yes, bless that world
this father's day.

STEPS

Yep. Can be awe inspiring
how the clouds back
and even pass over
trees, tree stumps, fallow
fields and spots of houses.
Lights and shadows step,
slip and slide this whole
county length, seen from
the width of ditch to ditch,
highway travels.

Small churches, groove
cut in pines 'lectric lines,
empty filling stations,
people at the mailboxes.
Time employed, this
tarnished land.
It's stark, yet hallowed,
 stretching, stepping,
and all still speaking
of a Beauty wept.

THE COURTSHIP

Doesn't *'Not a leg to stand on'*
suggest we're like some
species of shore bird
waiting on a tide to come,
or enrolled in a Yoga class
sweat pants equivalent,
and not just bipedal humans
facing some deserved judgment?

MORE ON PERMANENCE

Permanence is wider
than that pavement, and goes
along more varied than
any X of crossing roads, which is
just a thread and needle stitch,
patch on time's immortal passion,
the squeal of a semi's brake,
rumbling of acceleration:
seen, full well,
those smokey atoms--
scattered but eternal.

AT SANTEE WITH OLD JOHN

Not enough space here
to grace all grand things
beauty affords us. We
still have to bring
wide eyes for cathedrals,
tongue's hums for *Ahmen*s,
and limit discussion
to a whispered *of course*,
when we search the tall pines for
 Red-cockaded's choice.

SEWEE BAY: for Joel Munn

The twist and turn of labyrinthing,
the mystery where no question's been,
but tide was low then, now it's high,
Youth's channels laid in deep disguise
so where we thinks not where we are,
I once could do this in the dark.
Crab pots followed seems the best.
At least 'til Bay's eternal rest.

REFLECTIONS

All nature's gone to sleep:
even tooth, and even claw.
Sunk between the glistening eyes
and knobs of creature's nose,
asleep's the alligator's jaw.
And in wet quiet beauty grows.
Especially at the sky's toe holds.
It's kicked the covers back.

THURSDAY'S CHILD: THE CATARACTS

When the lights go dim
the house acquires
a dark decline.
Each step is from the higher:
a stair of chopped up line.
Still, go there little poem
on your paper airplane wings.
Sling yourself at shadows:
through the darkness spin.

WITH THE OLD GONE POET

Past classic columns, echoed lines,
down the slope to a poet's grave
the swats begin: the twisting dance…
in place of beauty, place of slave.

Camellias rise, a thicket grown.
Azaleas, dogwoods, all shorn
by summer's heat of joy. Employed
though in a nod to form.

Me swinging wild. Mosquitoes hum.
Houses do live. Houses die.
Gardens too, and words may try
but those words die. Still I

apply, nonetheless, myself,
to those same labors of the heart.
Follow poet and gardener's path:
by fallen petals shrug/smile. Start.

AN ECHAW REVERENCE

Ah, wondrous everything
that doesn't bite us or
make us itch: all wild
riches which we in idleness now
too thinly enjoy. Scale, feather,
hair of fur, each molecule in leaf,
flower, trunk or hanging branch
walked or paddled by, to y'all
let me, at least, give this small
but potent hymn of
a gently murmured hum…
plus, nod-like,
the occasional bow.

GARDEN NOTES

Reduced to nearly nothing.
Oh, look at me. An ink struck
paper thin being but, given
light and proper nutrients,
imagining he might here soon
unfold into a path edge bloom,
bright gleam of color: this
your nodding flower prayer.

AT HAMPTON PLANTATION

Within nature's great complexity
we questioning men or women are free to go,
in relative immunity—watch for snakes,
 and know the slopes of dark pine and oaks,
 sinks of cypress, tupelos, twisting creeks,
and shifting bright marsh,
to see a still nuthatch or blue tail skink
hold their link of branch, their strip of bark,
to regenerate with eyes an Eden,
Eden stacked and cantilevered,
Eden fielded or flower hidden.
But for tiredness and endless sinning,
Park's a camouflaged beginning.

BACK FROM THE DOCTOR

At my Uncle Wewa's fuel dock
we sold cans of *Esso* motor oil
and not just those: for a dime less
the recouped burnt stuff, *Actol*.
Same with sparkling *Coca Cola*.
Sold it and also *True Ade* which
is pale and squeezed from citrus peels.
Just so, old age has come to feel.
Only it's me buying.
Toting out the door
mild comforts of unreal.

AT THIS VERY MOMENT

If my father had lived he'd be 101
and I'd still be running to keep up.
As it is, many shuffling steps
may lean me that way just enough.

OF US TWO: for Lil.

Of us two let me be the tiredest,
the first to surrender, slip away,
close weary eyes, tilt head, and,
with a gentle snore, form
spittle on my lip's corner.

And you be the one to remove
this book from my hands,
to, with a smile of approval,
trace with your finger tip
the art work of the cover.

ON NATURE AND BEAUTY

Just consider us upon the landscape:
little round headed stick figure people
dwarfed by grand curly topped trees.
or thoroughly miniaturized when up
against some wavy lined ocean
and the page's nearly endless sky.
Now consider just beneath where arms
meet neck, the way our tiny hearts
keep gently beating—while a smiling
sun beams out her rays. On seeing,
little wonder dots for eyes grow wide.

ON VOYAGING: for Gwin

Pressed through surf
at each day's dawning,
oh, my heart's
a craft of longing.
Leapt aboard,
I raise bright sail.
I bring the scoop.
I'll need to bail.

ON PERSPECTIVE

Pole Yard evening's come.
Ibis hauled down golden sun.
They fixed the net to trailing feet,
then stroked their wings,
achieved a night. *Fait au complet.*
Ah, pretty done.
But as we speak of might,
these 'quitoes bring
grand moon so bright, and,
while they're pushing, sing.

ON LIFE AND DEATH

A brainpan's not a kettle.
More a tin pan, it would seem.
One to tap with finger,
an each man's tambourine.

The warbler comes a dancing
down from limb to limb,
through golden throat and open beak
sounds peeping wild thing's hymn.

At heart am I still frightened?
Well, I can't dance along.
Still inside hear me tapping,
rapt, lost in warbler's song.

PIED BEAUTY: AFTER HOPKINS

Grown weary of my aging,
yet this surprises me.
Cataracts have clouded eyes
'til I can only see
letters pressed and blurred.
Each word's a mystery.

Still from squinting, looking close,
a breathing pulse these take.
Some meaning's found in shapes.
Ink leaves on book stem shake,
and on the mind's a dappling
Life's lights and shadows make.

EXACTLY LIKE THIS

The trick when slightly lost
is to tote the sun over one
shoulder or the other
or at least keep the milky
promise of a sun
hovering there,
and use what breath
is spared to mutter
on where the truck belongs,
the prospect of oblivion,
or worse an anxious night
for wife at home. In just
minutes you've grown too old
to step and step and plunge,
breaking branches
as you come.
Yet at last, Oh, God
descends in wayward chance:
the path.

ON JEREMY CREEK

In heaven will I be allowed
to bog through salt marsh again?
Step down from the slant-poled, narrow
scrapped together gold plank walk, then
with mud sucking 'round my bare feet,
child's thin arms spread wide to steady,
head to the edge of a creek made of clouds?
The highest gulls are there already.

WHAT I LEARNED

Way back in century past, when I was
just a barefoot boy working
on that fuel dock and the phone
would ring, I'd snatch it up.
Sure enough, I'm running
to some boat. "Uncle We!
Long distance! Long distance!"
Even now, he's wiping
slick grease off his hands,
grinning, shaking his head,
saying: "Yep. Sure is."

THE LILIES AGAIN

I cross black coffee water
and lily pads between,
with desperate stumbling search
of mine confined to last night's dream.

Florescent bright the dragonflies
as sun's crept out from clouds,
and crowded lilies shine more white
exaggerated now.

No. Don't let me speak of wonder
for what can such praise mean?
Paddle raised, I smiling rip
momentum's pond dark seam.

CONSIDERING

To the Patient Ones

CONSIDERING

Guts in knots,
both eyes are going,
but still I hope for
morning poems

to pop like foam
on sunlit waves.
while high above
the gulls amaze

with pitching dives
of splendor spun,
a sparkle hefted,
hefted, flung,

as come what may
and come what might
mind's days still arc
of perfect light.

HEART

Thinking things in words,
we figure we must speak.
Yet hopes can pulse in silence.
Watch the quiet ones fish the creek

MY SESTINA.

Beyond the dawning sun
Time's zones long
since have run.
Sturdy lines of day begun
and day begun

stacked all the way to Spain,
where with lunch done, some
happy Spaniard uses tongue, lips
to spit the pit of Spanish olive
in their hand while thinking soon

a nap's to come, and not to be outdone,
first faced with morning sun,
I, weary Scot-Irish American,
plotted that same nap
for this afternoon.

MORE VILLAGE

To reach here
a century past,
you turned off a wide
but dirt King's Highway
where the small
rusted tin sign
nailed to a close hickory,
promised all travelers
who could read

"ASPRINOL IS BETTER
THAN WHISKEY!"

But in this recent
day and time,
none is still alive
to, by a rheumy
inner eye, trace
sign's simple boast
down the narrow lane
with its pine sap
scent and suggestion
of renewal.

IT'S HERE

There space enough
between print's lines,
where in the narrow
white goes unseen,
the laboring poet's
hidden message, which,
with fresh coffee scent,
sometime but not often,
is pure miraculous in the way
secret's been tapered to
a simple, final: *Finished*
it.

THE SHORTCUT

Do some paved corners of a mind
in time through use get shorted out?
Especially when past pain intrudes,
I've left the line a bit too soon.
Stepped away. Changed the route.
Worn dirt path by two feet wide,
Thought swamp daisies either side.
Don't ask me how among mind's stems
tossed plastic bottles chance to ride.

IMAGINE THIS

I won't mind.
Fold down the upper
corner of this page.
That way you can
come back maybe
days or only hours
from now, when
better rested or
less occupied, you
are purely ready
to walk this waiting
battered shore,
explore the waves
of tumbling waves and
taste gray salt.
All which is done
after tending
to the bend.
Smoothing
with your thumb.

AFTER THE MRI

About the ocean's water spouts,
they start from scratch, a wave
crest snatched, and suddenly the sky
is filled with anger of an unseen deep:
weeping funnel, shifting, bright,
a beauty sliced from rising light.
The same, of course, we keep inside,
down where the once dark things all hide.
Now lay back, float and close your eyes.

WHAT THE DOG AND I DISCUSSED

With dark eyes and flicking whiskers,
small gray squirrel, as if misgivings,
stops and looking back, sorta-kinda frowns
at feeder from which he's just jumped down.

A cringe of doubt? He's less assured
than when, with coming light, he leapt
and somehow kept the plastic squeezed,
to feed his greedy self on bird seeds.

Hells Bells. Can a squirrel know guilt?
Is he ashamed of theft? Ashamed we'll tell?
Or is nature's law mostly tooth and claw?
'least dogs and humans know guilt well.

ON PARADISE'S LIBRARY

Are there books in Heaven?
Crammed inside immense closet,
nest, chest of drawers, or cupboard?
Best of all the way Jorge Borges
has them shelved in an endless labyrinth.
And would even such be enough
to face bright endless nothingness?
If Love's around, with the right books
I might could.

AMONG THEM

Of course there's a glory
in many things, especially
the purposeful birds.
A heart stopping (ours),
head bobbing seeking
after sustenance,
with occasional raised wing-
adjustments Glory.
A Glory in trees, rivers,
rocks, seas. I like to think
even in the poem's abeyance
with its now stilled
lines maybe sacredly bled.
There's Glory here, and
we haven't died yet.

THOUGHTS ON CREMATION

There once was a pond
on wild Murphy Island's beach
just where the Santee reached
the sea. Slightly sickle shaped,
and high tide fed,
great spot-tailed bass
were this time led
into a long and shallow trap.
As water dropped their
panic spread. Guessed to be
a dozen plus, and each
three feet at least.
Fins revealed. Spotted tails
and sleek heads,
silver sided,
back and forth
they rushed, they glided.

So with little luck poaching ducks,
young I and friend thought it through:
Hell. Why not try
the high brass twos?
And went whooping, aiming, blaming,
all the while, running to keep up
but trailing bass.
Cut not one scale.

Failed at slaughter.
Still unrepentant,
I tore on. More life
of shouldn't oughtas,
shouldn't oughtas,
cracked, disordered.
'til in much needed
miracle of being,
flooding peace came 'round.

Same as surf pounds
wayward trees: oaks and cedars
skeletoned, stripped, gray. It's
fitting I'd be joining these.

PLUFF MUD: A VERSE

I've lost my youth. Don't ask me where.
Gone's every day right up 'til here.
Last I knew I'd propped my bike.
Woke bright morning bleary eyed, old
and wondering how I'd missed
 such a drastic ebbing tide.

The muddy sunken pulpwood sticks,
the ribs and keels of tilted crafts,
tossed rusty cables, engine blocks
pitched bottles, Actol cans, and done
oil filters from boats, cars, trucks,
 car bumper, too, the ripped tarred nets,
plus heaping strewn gray oyster shells.
Who'd guess the water fell so far
and how much stuff
that does not float.

Yet staring at that lost creek bed,
I am even more surprised
to find, set up within the mess,
a sparkling sheet tucked at my feet
and crumpled stretching to my chest,
while splashing at the window's
a gloried moment's morning sun.
I 'spect the time for smiling's come.

FULL DISCLOSURE

Half a long life ago I wrote a thick novel on what is
below. Condensed twelve years of work to these
few lines. Which is okay. From here I'll go to
heaven or I won't go. And, just so you know, in
the mid '80's I attended A.A. meetings in that
same Sunday School room as a child I'd mostly
been in. We even sat in the tiny chairs. It's what
we had, and by then nobody cared about such things.

Now:
Way, way back
my gentle granny said, "Oh, Land."
And the elder's fuss of God came down.
For hadn't she taken
His name in vain?
Lord and Land were close in sound.
She'd used the two in mocking exchange.
And the elders ran the Sunday School,
their struggle being with all ages:
to explain the Golden Rule.
Doing to others just might save us.
Anyway, I overheard
one say of David
after spying her bathing on the roof.
the King had sinned with poor Bathsheba.

Being six of age that's lost on me.
Was she named Bathsheba 'cause
of taking baths?
And who bathes on roofs? And what is sin
from which we're saved?
It's just as well. Sing Hallelujah.
Lord and Land and Land and Lord.
They did enough: Old Presbyterians.
All this stuff? You got it coming to ya.

GOOD MORNING

Being a plural proposition, I suppose
thinking 'bout the out of doors"
does require more than one white
colonial six-panel exterior right hinge
hung door to be flung open.
Well, magic coffee cup in hand,
I can expand on this poor single one,
flood the back wall with nothing but
wide doorways' lights. Brighten insides
'til tumbling thoughts have been reduced
to drifting dust motes, and such as plus
and minus are lost in an I forgot.

THE STUMP SQUAT'S TALE

The Twitcher and the Limbsit,
both vain as little birds can be,
decided on a sing off and to
judge they chose a Stump Squat: me.

I'd been deaf before their
births, just not letting on.
I'd tilt my hair tufted ears. Nail-
bitten talon tapped along.

Well-enough that got me by.
until this fateful day.
Not enough to close your eyes.
Who plays at hearing pays.

I won't bore you with my
poor acting or their loud,
much tortured songs. (Which I heard how?)
I'd watched the crowd.

The Flinches flinched
and Job O Links went off
to work, Soft Strummers
were the worst. They coughed.

Anyway, I did my best
at owl-like seeming wise.
A Solomon in Bird Land,
I called the thing a tie.

Neither the Twitcher or the
Limbsit is remotely satisfied.
Plus left my camera in the truck. (Damn the luck)
My judging them's unverified.

PASSAGE

As if the Devil left his wife
to tote the groceries,
as if the cold front cleared
his throat and spit is this
distant thunder plus a furious
drumming wet.

Not to put too keen a point on it:
a gully whumping bog strangling
rain, and yet I halt mid-slosh lost
in the time taken to watch a mass
of flooded fire ants float off,
as well as adjust my braces,
remove my glasses, and
with saturated sleeve wipe my face.

Then, supposed reasoning retrieved,
I make a mental note to bulk me up
as the *curious about nature* hero
in this my knot-like head's approaching
narrative flow.

NEAR DUTART CREEK

And when I do find a true forest primeval,
a woods unknown, a path which no one
took before, not even red men, women
and children, brave first humans with their
small spotted dogs. None of them. None.
Just quiet stepping wolves, and the stunted
bison found only east of the wide Mississippi
and, though they would not need a path,
passenger pigeons, so many they storm
 the sky with feathered thunders. There
both sides of the trail is thick with
rotted leaves, but further on harsh fires
caused by lightning strikes charred all, all's
fallen, and the fierce winds of hurricanes unnamed
crash the woods, and still the place renews.
And if and when I discover these things,
I will tie up yellow tapes. I will call to you.

WHAT KEEPS ME HERE

Said to date back to the days when
barbers did medical bloodletting,
the familiar poles still found in towns
feature bright interlocking red and white
spirals, lines at rare times even mechanized
into an endlessly rising barber advertising.
While here on this, sleepy to the point
 of being empty, country corner that design's
reduced to a flat peeling red paint, white paint,
red paint strip motionized with only the
rising, curling autumn variegated leaves
of Virginia creeper, which maybe could be
an old heart's message to the world.

ON TURNING THIRTY-SIX

Did you start flipping from the back?
If so, relax. I admit it. Even poets
on occasion do the same No fault. No blame.
No surprise. You've quickly seen what's coming.
Though you should know found in this very book
is a front to back pacing. A built in growing
understanding of all place and time,
of form, shape, sound, sense and rhyme.
Let tired me, laughing, boast.
A proper going can bring a special wisdom--
even if it's acquired in thirty minutes. From
here on resist first impulse. Turn around. Never too late.
Let's say life's a small dusty carnie midway.
Peanut shells beneath your feet, start here. Retreat
into this musty, tender, greedy hall of mirrors.
Face up. Grin and bear it.
Smile, embrace.

OF BIBLICAL PROPORTIONS

Before plunging down the sidewalk,
I waited for the silver gray clouds
to bank themselves, for the dreary rain
to truly threaten. Then thoughts crowded
with a foregone drenching set off toward
the waterfront where sure enough
many warm drops soon sopped
their way through clothes to skin
to surprisingly bring, if not exactly
ecstasy, a comfortable intimacy
with everything which ever was
when I was young.

The smell of cigarettes they smoked.
The click of whiskey drunk. Soft
drumming on the sleeping porch
when the afternoon storm comes
with its damp warmth of the rain's sheet
and the smudged light finds the sagging dock
containing all that floats, that needs to float,
the seemingly abandoned boats,
palmettos rattling their psalms,
and a creaking oil sign.

Next the soaking wet churches, houses,
twisting moss trimmed oak limbs,
these objects of the streets seen
from the steamy inside of a hissing
'50's darkly painted roach-shaped car..
The there of there there, there, there.
Me riding barefoot. Rain is everywhere.

And so it goes to be surprised
by this my implied baptism.
Old honey, locust eating John
standing in the River Jordan could have
done no better. I'd have been no wetter.
Thus blessed and, as much as a seventy-
seven year old can be, transformed,
I cleaning glasses, straightening stance,
squishing but with a light step,
turn for home.

PROTHONOTORY: LOVE POEM

Sure there may be more to it. But, oh,
hardly a secret, my job as poet
is in part, as the Mississippi sage had it,
"to raise up the hearts of men and women."
I hear you saying "Done in his case
by reporting, yet again, on that same
woods 'round a forty acre lily pond."
(I can hear me say it 'bout myself.) Yes. But
wet grounds where tan-gray wide based
cypress and tupelos renew themselves
though sometimes not. A woods where.
small golden-warrior-warblers
and equally-consistent-female-mates
through dipping limbs do acrobatics.
But actually these I speak of recently flew
down to South America,
where they stay 'til spring brings 'em
back to flirt, flit and sing chirping
songs of pure romance. Scuffling males
collide mid air. Then once paired, future parents
nest in well-selected rotted hollow trees
and stumps and cypress knees. Even wood duck boxes.

Eggs hatch. And through a constant
ferrying of grubs and insect heads, trunks and legs
their fuzzy pink gray rubbery young
are fed to a slight maturity. Bird children
which quickly enter beside them
in a pliable, but swiftly ruthless
world of odds defying true endurance,
all the while supplying what we humans
think we know of beauty.

SCHOOL DAYS

These messages that came at dawn
the roar of chainsaw being drawn
low across the big pine's trunk.
The creak, crack, thump that makes a stump.
And warmed on coals from smoky sticks
a chicken bog, canned collards lunch.
Lost in blue smoke black men ghosts.
Lost in time. And high school me?
My job's to pump-spray a deadly
poison on each fresh cut stump,
while my lunch break's done in a tin
boat floating on a mile away lake...
staring into an August sun. Concerning
life there's some mistake. To then have taken
myself in hand? Would that be wrong? Or so
he'd scratch down long years on.

DOG SONG 119

When you were alive ventriloquist me and you
often had conversations of some importance:
meals, naps, being old, what the damn cats had done.
Once when you were dead, I tried again. Inquired
how you passed the hours? You just said,
"It's a field filled with broom sedge and
small wild flowers." I realized then
you must be young and could run.

OH

When writing poetry
the benefit of the doubt
is about the last thing
I want to give up. Without
doubt a boring precision's
needed when going mouth
to ear or in the mind's fast
snap to snap route.
But some pronounce route root.
See how quick this gets trickier.
Seems deliberately obtuse. But
it's just playing fast and loose
with words whose clout's
been clotted to the point
in the dairy shouts
are herd. No longer
content, brown cows
udderly abandon
reason…
for now.

COFFEE SONG

No comment for the first cup drunk
A usual morning's curtain's rent.
Nothing else. Well, a breath is
expelled with each inhaling.
And…maybe, just maybe,
each of these is slightly sweeter
air warmer, more precious
than most taken by this same breather
up' til then. Are hopes numbered?
On the kitchen clock's time shredder face
the quick long slicing hand is driven
by the stout one's mock languid pace.
and unrealizing me is pleased enough
with a second cup.

ON ORANGE

Orange and pink
make a mess in the sink,
joined by orange and blue:
a purplish wasted stew.
But wait. Orange and tan
rhymes with orangutan,
which orange couldn't
do without the tan: that is.
hang by one hand
in a far off wild wood
and fear only man.

&

THE BIG ONE

Eternal starts with A,B.C and goes past Z
eternally. Same with numbers: 1,2,3 but
there kazillion takes the place of Z.
Hope that's helped you see what's what.
Tuesday, Wednesday, buckle my shoe.
Put's endless end to what is not.

ON TIME AND LIFE'S ERRANDS

How few among the trillions
these grains of sand beneath
my heels, between my toes.
Enough to hold me upright though,
and when I turn away, to lever me
in giant step. I haven't come down yet.
But met the gulls high eye to eye.
And spoke to them in language where
what's in the past can play no part,
for nothing done or been can start.
In the sky are no regrets. Of course,
I'm thinking had we some,
I'd cease to treat these arms
like wings.

AT THE FORD'S TAILGATE

I'm ready for the world, at least
the Southern dirt road part. Eye,
ear, foot, hand and heart…and
yes, a healthy jolt of luck.
All I need's a woman's touch:
your push to help me start this truck.

KITE EXUBERANCE : UNFINISHED

No matter how still the blue appears,
trust a breeze to stir up there.
No bird soars in what is still.
He tilts his wings, brings will
to bare on this wide Delta sky.
And just one swallow-tail to fly,
ignoring marsh, which seems to crawl,
then plunging, twisting, dexterous fall
stuns us all, brings laughter's bliss.
Wild beauty traced with eyes as if...

THE WAY

The treacherous path I keep inside,
sweet tried and true I've yet to try.
the second step with three nails loose,
the moral slope where I can slide,

That short cut through not put to use,
me guessing who is living proof,
the dream I'll need if I'm to sleep,
patched ladder leaning 'gainst the roof.

EDISTO AGAIN

Nothing pure gold
will stay awake.
Real silver sleeps
make no mistake.
You want what lasts,
then make it vast,
some rolling ocean,
something grand,
spending passion
on wet sand.

Which a child will
heap to castle. And
bowing, leaping
little dog barks
what, of course, are
joy's remarks.
Plastic shovel.
Banged bright can.
Reaching child
with reaching hand.

DEAR LORD,

I've tired my blood, gastrics too. The
brain can't maintain when I stand
fine fluid *balances* of youth.
Well oiled motions grind in time, and
breathes once held self-evident,
in truth, despite prime savings plan,
through the years these came and went.
But who are we to make demand?
Yet fetch with Love another start.
Please this morning stretch our hearts.

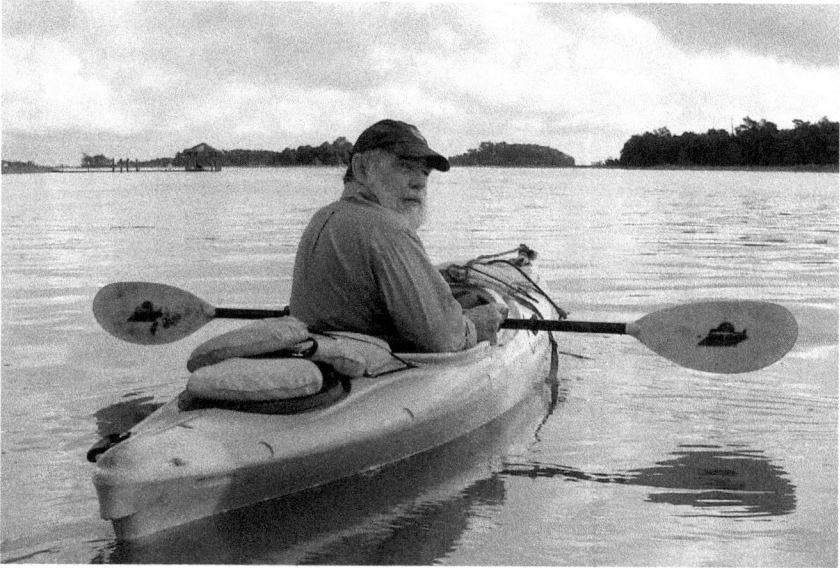

photo by S. Hindman

A lifelong resident of the Carolina Low Country, William P. Baldwin is an award-winning novelist, poet, biographer and historian. He graduated from Clemson with a BA in History and an MA in English. He ran a shrimp boat for nine years then built houses, but the principle occupation of his life has been writing.

His works include the popular oral histories *Mrs. Whaley and Her Charleston Garden* and, with Genevieve "Sister" Peterkin, *Heaven is a Beautiful Place*. The screen play for the latter earned him a Silver Remy at the Houston Film Festival. *Journey of a Hope Merchant*, the life of around the world solo sailor Neal Petersen, won the National Outdoor Writing Award. For its depiction of Southern race relations his first novel *The Hard to Catch* won the Lillian Smith Award . He wrote three more. *Charleston Magazine* called Baldwin's latest, *Charles Town*, "a robust, self-confident conglomeration of sophistication, bawdiness, and bravado…a tour de force."

With photographer V. Elizabeth Turk he did *Mantelpieces of the Old South* and supplied the text for chef Charlotte Jenkin's *Gullah Cuisine*. He collaborated with architectural photographer N. Jane Iseley on *Charleston, Charleston Impressions, Daytrips from Charleston, Plantations of the Low Country*, and *Low Country Plantations Today*.

Done with photographer Selden Hill and published in 2011, *The Unpainted South* won the Gold Benjamin Franklin Award for poetry given by the Independent Book Sellers Association. The follow up collection *These Our Offerings* earned a second Benjamin Franklin Award. Both were published with Evening Post Books.

And most recently Class Publishing brought out *Carolina Rambling: a Visual and Poetical Tour*. A fine match to the earlier two, this collection features Selden Hill's color photography. A beautiful book!

Baldwin's writing has also appeared in *Charleston, Garden and Gun, Southern Living, Victoria, Veranda, Southern Accents, Grace, Humans and Nature* magazines, *the Atlanta Constitution,* and on the electronic poetry site: *Poem du jour*.